UNDERSTANDING
----- OUR -----
SKELETON

LUCY BEEVOR

capstone

Edited by Brenda Haugen
Designed by Russell Griesmer and Jennifer Bergstrom
Original illustrations © Capstone Global Library Limited 2016
Picture research by Jo Miller
Production by Jennifer Bergstrom
Originated by Capstone Global Library Limited

Library of Congress Cataloging-in-Publication Data
Names: Beevor, Lucy, author.
Title: Understanding our skeleton / by Lucy Beevor.
Description: North Mankato, Minnesota : Heinemann Raintree, a Capstone
 imprint, [2017] | Series: Raintree perspectives. Brains, body, bones! |
 Audience: Ages 8-11. | Audience: Grades 4 to 6. | Includes bibliographical
 references and index.
Identifiers: LCCN 2016036123|
ISBN 9781410985781 (library binding) |
ISBN 9781410985828 (paperback) |
ISBN 9781410985941 (eBook PDF)
Subjects: LCSH: Human skeleton—Juvenile literature. | Bones—Juvenile
 literature. | Human anatomy—Juvenile literature.
Classification: LCC QM101 .B44 2017 | DDC 611/.71—dc23
LC record available at https://lccn.loc.gov/2016036123

Acknowledgments
We would like to thank the following for permission to reproduce photographs: Getty Images: NYPL NYPL, 23; Newscom: Blend Images/Erik Isakson, 25; Shutterstock/Alila Medical Media, 9, 10 (top), Arcady, 7, Blamb, 19, DuToVision, 6, eAlisa, 17, Greg Epperson, 27, illustrart, 15, Kameel4u, 20, Kniazeff, 29, NoPainNoGain, 13, Puwadol Jaturawutthichai, 24, Reha Mark, cover, Robyn Mackenzie, 18, sciencepics, 21, Sebastian Kaulitzki, 5, 10 (bottom left and right), 12, tose, 16, Vectomart, 22; design elements: Shutterstock: designelements, PILart, Ohn Mar, sir_Enity, Studio_G, WINS86

Every effort has been made to contact copyright holders of material reproduced in this book. Any omissions will be rectified in subsequent printings if notice is given to the publisher.

All the internet addresses (URLs) given in this book were valid at the time of going to press. However, due to the dynamic nature of the internet, some addresses may have changed, or sites may have changed or ceased to exist since publication. While the author and publisher regret any inconvenience this may cause readers, no responsibility for any such changes can be accepted by either the author or the publisher.

TABLE OF CONTENTS

Some words are shown in bold, **like this**. You can find out what they mean by looking in the glossary.

A SOLID FRAMEWORK

Imagine a skyscraper made without a framework of steel. Would the building hold up against a bad storm? Sturdy frameworks give buildings shape and provide support. The 206 bones of your skeleton provide the framework for your body. Without a skeleton, you would be a shapeless blob. Your height, shape, and the length of your limbs all depend on your skeleton.

Together with your muscles, your skeleton helps you to move. But that's not all it does. The skeleton is a living part of your body. Deep inside, your bones make blood cells that keep you healthy. By itself, a skeleton might look a little scary, but it's not at all. The human skeleton is an amazing combination of strength and balance.

Muscles keep our skeleton in an upright position and help us to move.

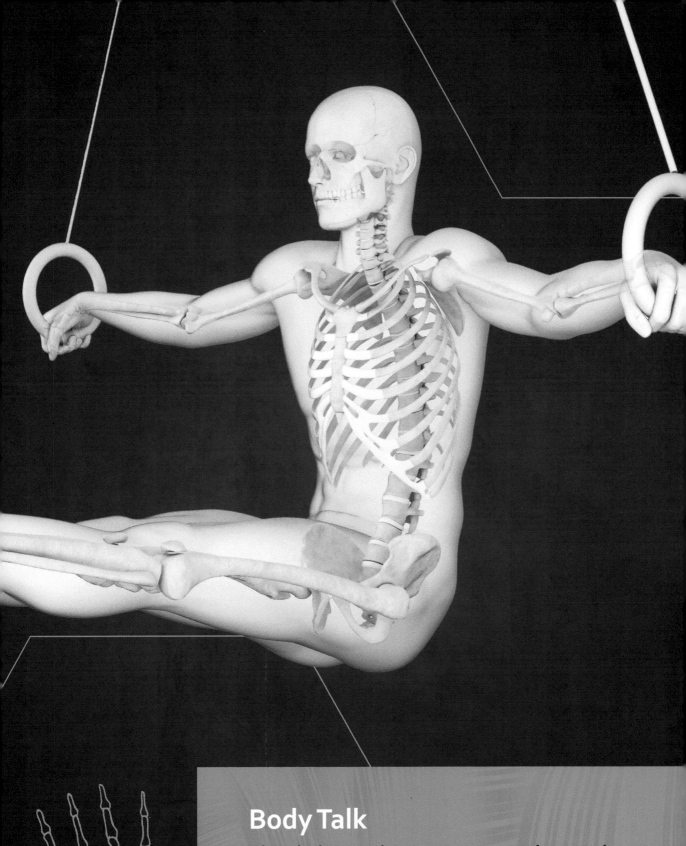

Body Talk

The skeleton also protects your *internal* organs. For example, your bones form a cage around your lungs and heart.

UNDER THE SKIN

Bones don't just lie underneath the skin. Your skeleton is hidden beneath muscles and connective **tissues**. The tissues attach bones to muscles and other bones.

Tendons and ligaments are tough, cord-like connective tissues. Ligaments hold your bones together so they don't pop out of place. Tendons attach muscles to bones. Flexing a muscle pulls on the tendon, like a bungee cord. Then the tendon pulls on the bone to move it. When you flex your upper arm muscle—the biceps—strong tendons pull your forearm up.

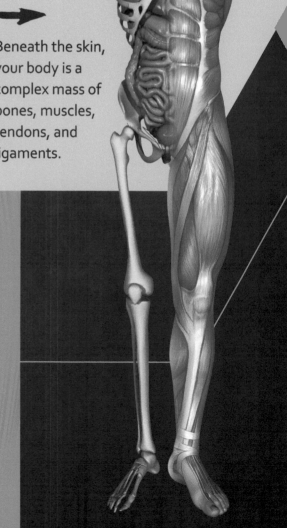

Beneath the skin, your body is a complex mass of bones, muscles, tendons, and ligaments.

Body Talk

When a bone is broken, it regrows and repairs itself. A doctor will put a cast or a *splint* on a broken bone to help the bone grow straight and stay in the right position.

nose

See for Yourself

Rub your nose, and gently wiggle it. Does it feel squishy at the end? That's because there isn't a bone at the end of the nose. You can feel where your nose bone ends and your cartilage begins.

Cartilage adds padding between bones to protect them from rubbing together. This strong, rubbery tissue also gives shape where there are no bones. Your outer ears and the lower half of your nose are made of cartilage.

Where Bones Get Together

If you could look under all those connective tissues, you would see how your bones fit together. The place where two or more bones meet is called a joint. Without joints, you wouldn't be able to jump, run, or move at all. You can move because of your joints and the muscles that power them.

Protective *capsules* surround moving joints. These capsules are filled with a thick, slippery fluid known as *synovial fluid*. The fluid helps to keep joints moving smoothly and also stops them from rubbing together and wearing away. For even more protection, the ends of the bones are padded with cartilage.

Body Talk

The hyoid is the only bone that does not connect to any other bones in the body, because it doesn't have any joints. This small horseshoe-shaped bone is instead anchored by muscles and ligaments at the base of the tongue. It helps you to move your tongue, swallow, and produce your voice.

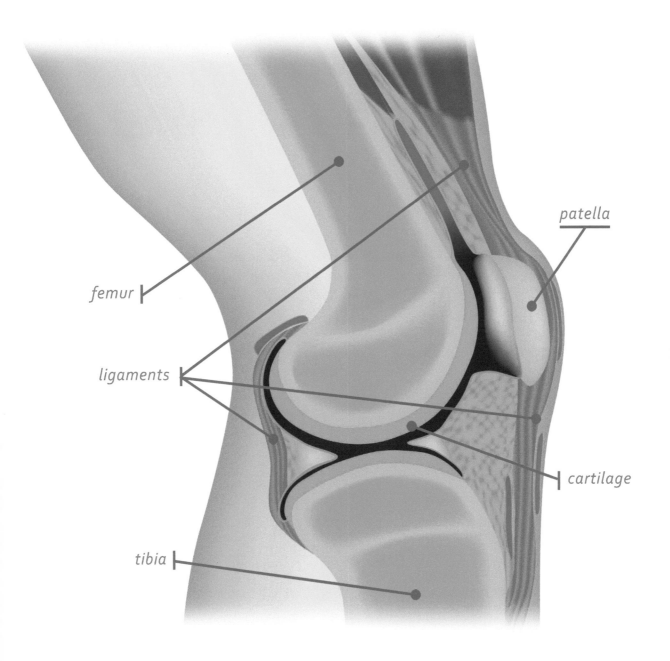

patella

femur

ligaments

cartilage

tibia

 The knee is the largest joint in the body and also the most complicated.

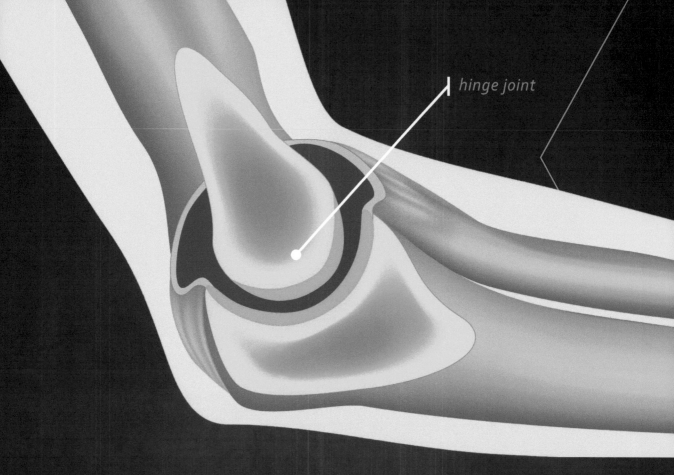

hinge joint

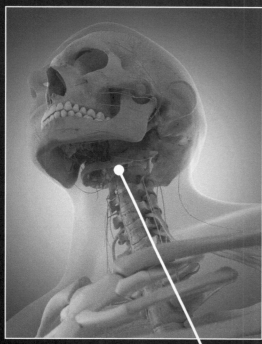

pivot joint

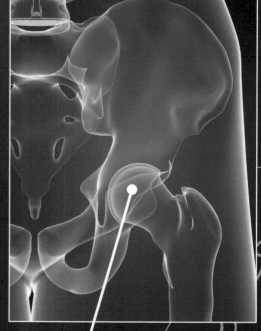

ball-and-socket joint

Move your body
to see these
different joints
in action.

A Joint Effort

The many joints of your skeleton allow you to move in different ways. Each type of joint is named for what it looks like or how it works.

Ball-and-socket joints allow bones to move in all directions. The rounded head of one bone fits into the hollow space, or socket, of another. In your hip, the head of the femur (thighbone) fits into a socket in the *pelvis*.

Hinge joints move bones forward and backward only. These joints join two bones together like a door hinge. Your knees and elbows have hinge joints.

In a pivot joint, one ring-shaped bone turns around another cylinder-shaped bone. The head and neck form a pivot joint. This joint allows you to turn your head from side to side.

A Perfect Fit

Each bone in your body is shaped perfectly for the job it does. In fact, your skeleton is like a giant jigsaw puzzle of bones that fit together in amazing ways. Your spine is made of round bones that bend and twist at their joints. Arm and leg bones are rounded at the ends so they move smoothly against each other. Other bones, such as shoulder blades and hip bones, are large and flat. This shape allows them to attach firmly to the strong muscles that move your arms and legs.

BARE BONES

Once you get past muscles and connective tissues, you're left with the bare bones. Tap on the top of your head. Pretty solid, right? Skull bones form a "helmet," which protects your brain. You can't move these bones. Of the 29 bones that make up your skull, only the lower jawbone moves.

Leading down from your skull, your spine is strong and tall like a tree trunk. It is made up of 26 bumpy bones, which fit together to support your body. They also protect your *spinal cord*.

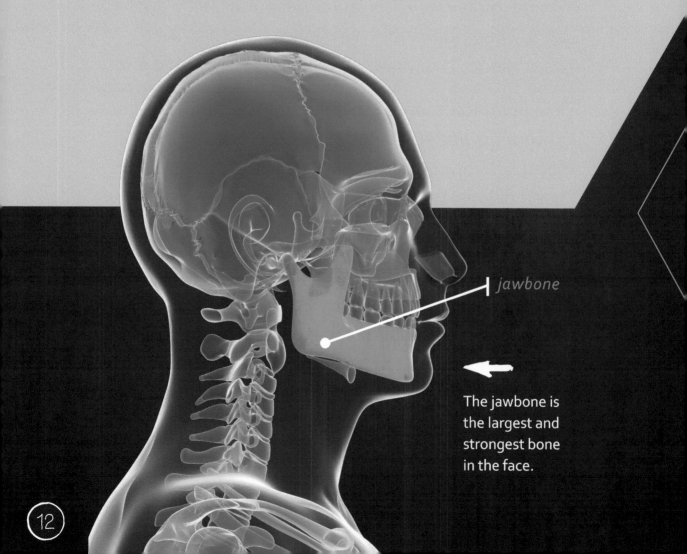

jawbone

The jawbone is the largest and strongest bone in the face.

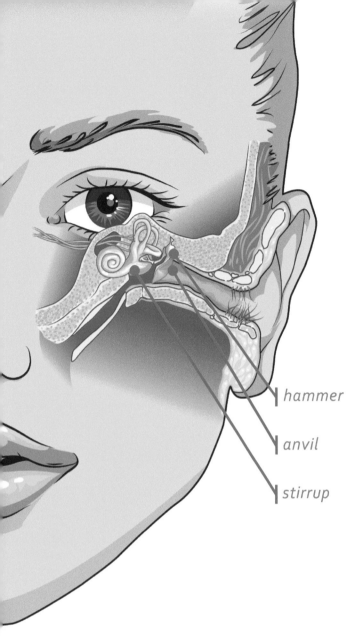

Tiny but Mighty

Your skull contains the six smallest bones in the human body. Deep inside your ear are three tiny bones called the hammer, anvil, and stirrup. They are named for their shapes. These bones may be tiny, but they do a big job. They help carry sound waves to the brain.

hammer

anvil

stirrup

The stirrup in the inner ear is the smallest bone in the body. It measures roughly 0.12 x 0.1 inch (3 x 2.5 millimeters).

See for Yourself

Take a deep breath. Did your ribs move? Your 24 ribs are connected by cartilage that keeps them in place to protect your lungs. But the cartilage also stretches so that your ribs can move just enough to allow your lungs to fill with air.

Arms Wide Open

Your arms connect to your skeleton at your shoulders. Scapulas, or shoulder blades, have round grooves where the upper arm bones fit. The clavicle, or collarbone, is shaped like a long "S" to hold your shoulder joints away from the trunk of your body. This allows you to move your arms in more ways.

The humerus is the long bone that runs from your shoulder to your elbow. Have you ever bumped that spot on your elbow that makes your arm feel numb? People call that hitting your "funny bone." But really it's a nerve in your elbow that causes the loss of feeling.

The two bones of your lower arm, the radius and ulna, do a cool trick. When your palm faces up, the bones run side by side. When your palm faces down, they form an "X" as one bone flips over the other. These bones make turning a doorknob possible.

Body Talk

Your arm only has three bones, but your little wrist has eight. They allow you to move your wrist in all directions.

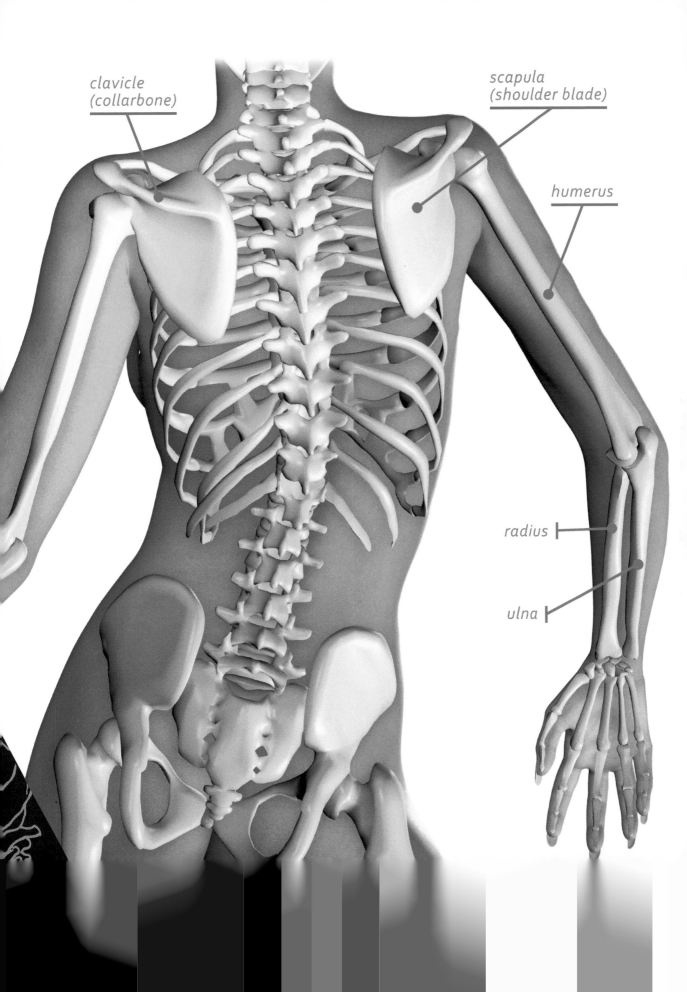

clavicle
(collarbone)

scapula
(shoulder blade)

humerus

radius

ulna

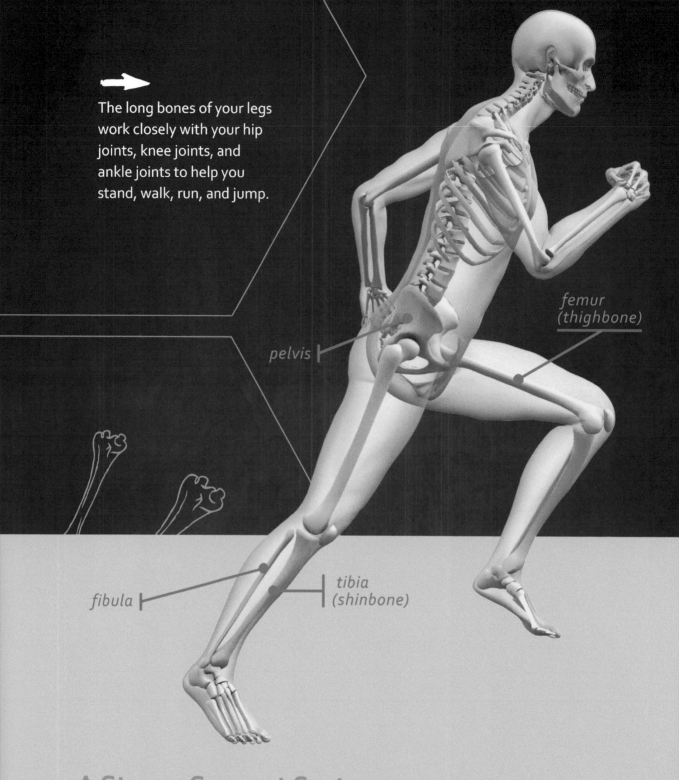

The long bones of your legs work closely with your hip joints, knee joints, and ankle joints to help you stand, walk, run, and jump.

femur (thighbone)

pelvis

fibula

tibia (shinbone)

A Strong Support System

Every day your pelvis carries a lot of weight. Sitting, standing, even lying down, your pelvis helps to support you. Its wide, curved shape cradles your *torso*. This shape also allows you to walk on two legs.

The farther down your body you go, the more weight that part of the skeleton supports. Running and jumping put a lot of stress on the leg bones. The thick bones of the legs are very strong. Your femurs are the longest and heaviest bones in your body. Buried deep in muscles, the femur is one of the few bones you can't feel through your skin. Below the knee joint, there are two bones that make up your lower leg—the tibia and fibula. Of the two, the tibia, or shinbone, is the largest. In fact, it is the second-longest bone in the body.

But your legs don't do all the work. With each step, your feet support all of your weight. The arching shape of the foot is the best shape for supporting weight. That's why architects use the arch design to add strength to their structures.

Most people have arches in the bottoms of their feet, but some do not. This is known as fallen arches or flat feet. It's usually not too serious, but fallen arches can sometimes lead to foot, leg, hip, and/or lower back issues. Wearing supportive shoes with specially made insoles can help to support the feet and prevent pain.

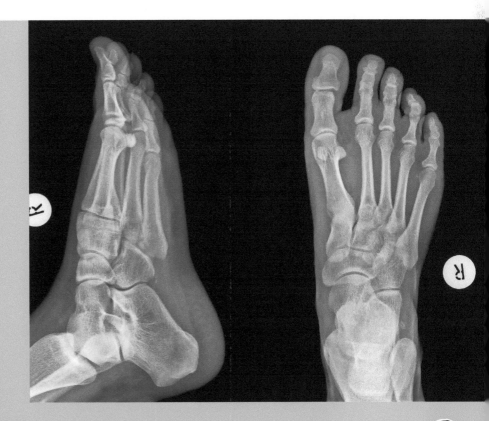

A CLOSER LOOK AT BONE

From the top of your skull to the tips of your toes, your skeleton is an engineering wonder. But inside those hard bones is a whole world of activity.

If you could peel back the smooth surface of a bone, you would find a thick layer of compact bone. It is the heaviest, hardest type of bone. It is made up of **calcium** and strong, bendy **collagen**. Calcium makes bones hard. Collagen makes bones hard to break. Compact bone provides protection and support to the layers underneath. About 80 percent of the bones in the body are compact bone.

Foods such as milk, cheese, yogurt, leafy greens, and almonds are good sources of calcium. All of these foods help your bones to stay strong.

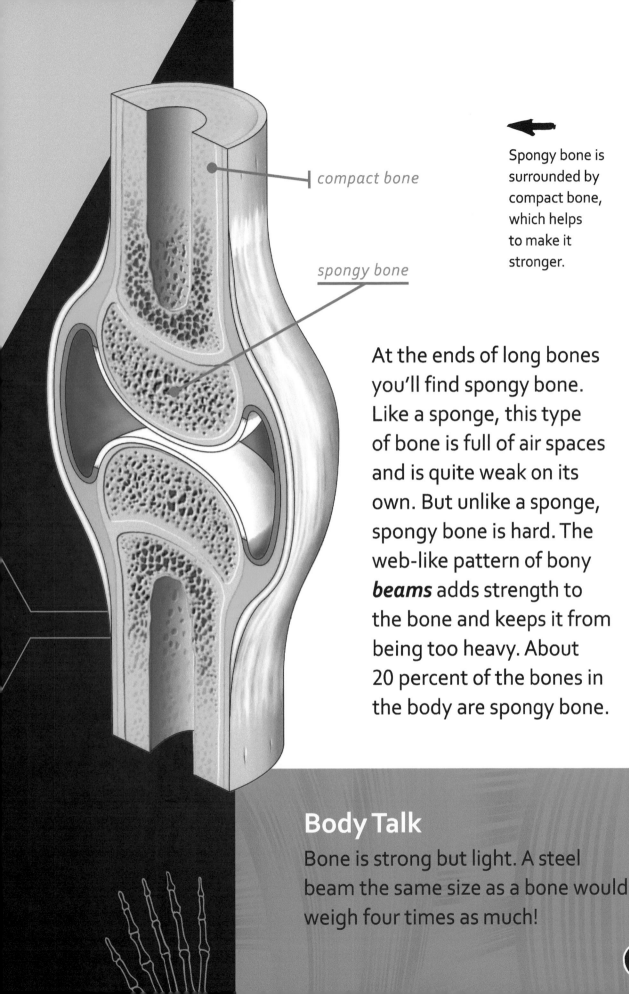

compact bone

spongy bone

Spongy bone is surrounded by compact bone, which helps to make it stronger.

At the ends of long bones you'll find spongy bone. Like a sponge, this type of bone is full of air spaces and is quite weak on its own. But unlike a sponge, spongy bone is hard. The web-like pattern of bony **beams** adds strength to the bone and keeps it from being too heavy. About 20 percent of the bones in the body are spongy bone.

Body Talk

Bone is strong but light. A steel beam the same size as a bone would weigh four times as much!

Crack!

If you break a bone, your doctor will put it in a plaster cast or splint. But the cast just keeps everything in place. The bone itself does the work of healing. When a bone breaks, bone cells gather around the break and make *callus*. Over time, the bone cells make strong bone material from the callus. Bones heal at different rates, depending on the patient's age and where the break is. But from around 6 weeks to 3 or 4 months, the bone is as good as new again.

← Once the bone is healed, doctors use a small electric saw to remove the cast. It sounds scary, but the saw's blade isn't actually sharp. It moves from side to side, so the vibrations cut the cast. It's quick and painless and may even tickle!

blood vessels

Every second, bone marrow produces about 2 million red blood cells.

bone marrow

spongy bone

compact bone

Living Bones

Although we often think of bones as non-living objects, they are actually living, growing tissue. Inside the compact bone, tiny tubes run the length of the bone. The tubes contain blood vessels that supply blood and oxygen to the bone cells.

Deep inside, the centers of your large bones are fairly hollow. This hollow space is called the marrow cavity. Compared with the smooth, white outer bone, the marrow cavity looks fuzzy and red. But this isn't just empty space. Inside the marrow cavity, jelly-like bone marrow does important work. Bone marrow makes blood cells that carry oxygen through the body and fight infection. It also makes cells called platelets that help blood to **clot**.

Bone Growth

You have your bones to thank each time you grow out of your favorite jeans. The ends of your long bones, such as those in your arms and legs, contain small amounts of cartilage. The cartilage slowly turns to bone as you get older. As long as there is cartilage, the bone continues to grow. By the time you are an adult, all the cartilage is replaced by bone. Your bones then stop growing.

Bones grow thicker too. Special cells build bone layers from the outside in. But the marrow cavity also needs to grow. Other cells break down bone from the inside. As the bones grow on the outside, the inside breaks down to keep the bone at just the right thickness.

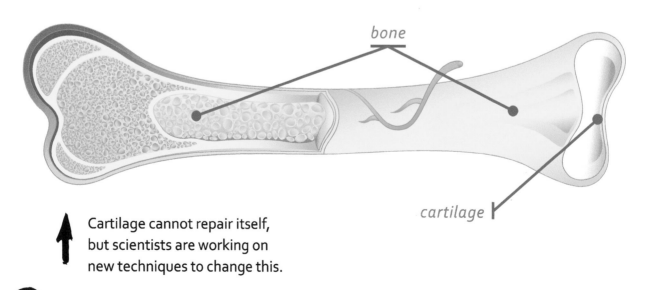

bone

cartilage

Cartilage cannot repair itself, but scientists are working on new techniques to change this.

The Giant of Illinois

The tallest man in recorded history was Robert Pershing Wadlow (1918–1940). Born in Illinois, Wadlow grew to an amazing 8 feet 11.1 inches (2.72 meters). He became a celebrity and was nicknamed "the Giant of Illinois." But being that tall was tough. Wadlow had to wear special leg braces to support his legs and had little feeling in his feet. His height put a lot of stress on his body, but Wadlow led a mostly healthy life and still has his place in the record books today.

A HEALTHY SKELETON

Your bones take care of you if you take care of them. A healthy diet is important for bone health. Calcium and vitamin D help to keep your bones healthy and strong. Milk and other dairy products are good sources of these important nutrients, as are leafy greens such as broccoli and kale. Sunlight is also a good source of vitamin D.

Your bones can take a lot of stress, but they do have their breaking points. How easily a bone can break, or fracture, depends on diet, physical condition, health, and age. The bones of children don't break as easily as those of older people. Children's bones also heal faster when they do break.

 You can break a bone in a fall or on impact. Some diseases that weaken the bones, such as osteoporosis, can also cause fractures.

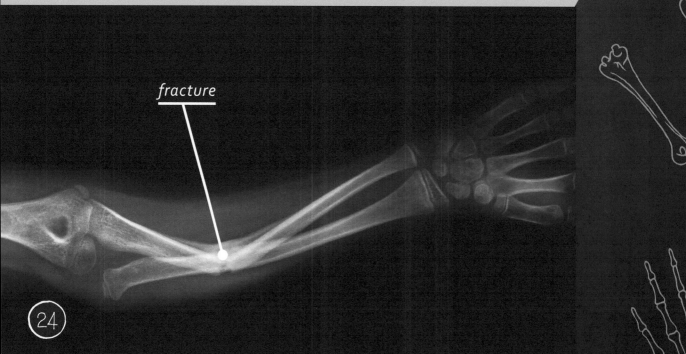

fracture

Exercise, even daily walks, helps to make bones stronger and healthier.

Strong on the Inside

You know that exercise makes your muscles bigger and stronger. But did you know that your bones also respond to exercise? Exercise increases blood flow, which helps bones to grow thicker and stronger. Athletes and people who do heavy work have thicker bones. Ballet dancers, who spend lots of time on their toes, develop slightly larger toe bones.

Body Talk

We are born with many more bones structures than we have as adults. Newborn babies have more than 300 bone and cartilage structures. As we grow, some of these fuse together into bigger, stronger bones, so that by adulthood we are left with the 206 bones that make up the human skeleton.

Super Skeleton

Your incredible skeleton is always working. It keeps you strong and on the move. Whether you are standing, sitting, or running, your skeleton gives you support and protection. Your spine is working hard to hold your body upright, and your ribs are protecting your heart and lungs. Your legs provide strength and your feet support. Even if you are lying perfectly still, your tiny ear bones are working, sending sound to your brain.

Your bones are stronger than steel but still light enough to let you move around. Many features of the skeleton have been copied to build better buildings and other structures. But no structure could ever match the wonders of the human skeleton.

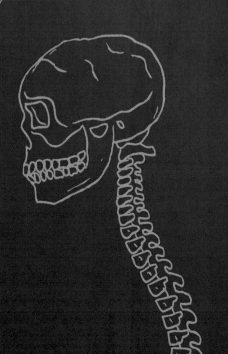

↑ The hands and feet contain over half the body's bones. Each hand has 27 bones, and each foot has 26, making 106 in total!

SEE INSIDE:
THE SKELETON

A   **SKULL** Your face has 14 bones.

B   **JAWBONE** The jawbone holds your lower teeth in place.

C   **SPINE** The 26 bones of the spine are called vertebrae.

D   **RIBS** Most people have 12 pairs of rib bones, but a few people have an extra pair.

E   **PELVIS** The *pelvis* is made of six bones joined together.

F   **FEMUR** The femur makes up about one-fourth of your total height.

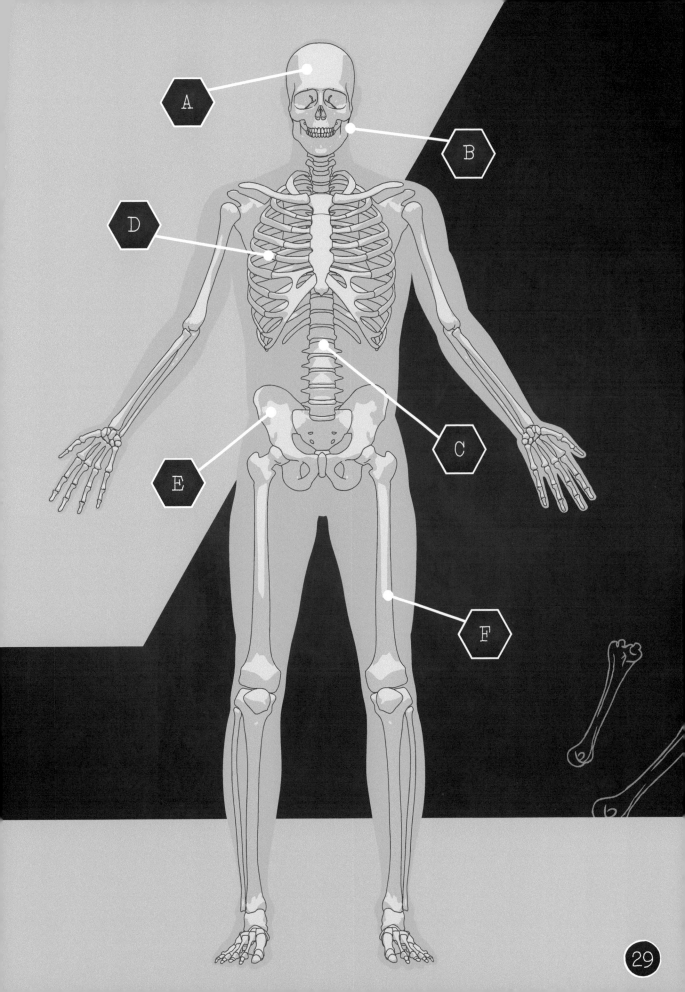

GLOSSARY

beam (BEEM)—sturdy structure that provides support

calcium (KAL-see-uhm)—soft mineral needed for strong teeth and bones

callus (KA-luhs)—bony tissue that forms around the end of a healing bone

capsule (KAP-suhl)—tough membrane that encloses something in the body

clot (KLOT)—become thicker and more solid; blood clots stop the body from bleeding

collagen (KALL-uh-jen)—protein found in connective tissues, skin, and bones

internal (in-TUR-nuhl)—inside the body

limb (LIM)—part of a body used in moving or grasping; in the human body, a limb is an arm or leg

pelvis (PEL-viss)—large bony structure near the base of the spine where the legs attach

spinal cord (SPY-nuhl KORD)—thick cord of nerve tissue in the neck and back; the spinal cord links the brain to the body's other nerves

splint (SPLINT)—strip of rigid material used to support a broken bone when healing

synovial fluid (suh-NO-vee-uhl FLOO-id)—smooth, clear liquid that helps to keep joints moving properly

tissue (TISH-yoo)—collection of cells that makes up the body; tissues perform different actions

torso (TOR-soh)—part of the body between the neck and waist, not including the arms

READ MORE

Brown, Carron, and Rachael Saunders. *The Human Body*. Shine-a-Light. Tulsa, Okla.: Kane Miller Books, 2016.

Mason, Paul. *Your Strong Skeleton and Amazing Muscular System.* Your Brilliant Body. New York: Crabtree Publishing, 2016.

Morgan, Ben, Steve Parker, and Edwood Burn. *The Skeleton Book.* New York: DK Kids, 2016.

INTERNET SITES

FactHound offers a safe, fun way to find Internet sites related to this book. All of the sites on FactHound have been researched by our staff.

Here's all you do:

Visit *www.facthound.com*

Type in this code: 9781410985781

Super-cool stuff! Check out projects, games and lots more at
www.capstonekids.com

INDEX